LET'S
STAY-AT-HOME
GAMES

TORMONT

Research and games: Diane Mineau
Text adaptation: Catherine Solyom
Graphic design: Zapp
Illustrations: Fred Schrier and André Morin

© 1998 Tormont Publications Inc.
338 Saint Antoine St. East
Montreal, Canada H2Y 1A3
Tel. (514) 954-1441
Fax (514) 954-5086

The publisher thanks Heritage Canada for the
support awarded under the Book Publishing
Industry Development Program.

Printed in China

CONTENTS

Mini-Solitaire

Number of Players: 1

What You Need:
- the Mini-Solitaire game board
- 20 counters

RULES OF THE GAME

1 Place a counter on each circle of the game board, except for the one in the centre.

2 For each turn, you must capture a counter by jumping over it with another counter. You can jump horizontally or vertically, but you must always land on an empty circle. Remove the counters that you capture from the game board.

4

Object of the Game:
to capture as many counters
as possible.

3 Continue playing until you can no longer move. Count all the
captured counters and play again to see if you can capture
even more.

Variation: play by the same rules but try to end up with your last
counter on the circle at the centre of the game board.

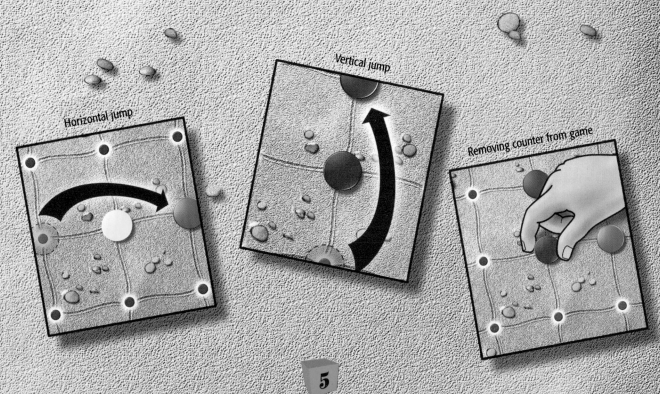

Horizontal jump

Vertical jump

Removing counter from game

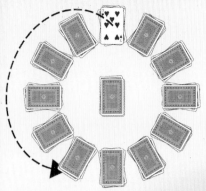

THE
King's Clock

Number of Players: 1

What You Need:
- 52 playing cards

Object of the Game:
to turn over all the cards and place them in the right place on the clock before you turn over the 4 Kings.

RULES OF THE GAME

1 Make sure you have removed the jokers from the deck. Shuffle the cards well.

2 Place 12 cards face down on the table in a circle, to form the face of a clock. Place another card face down in the centre. With the remaining cards, place them face down around the clock until there are no cards left. Don't forget to put a card in the centre each time you go around the clock.

3 Turn over the card on the top of the pile at 12 o'clock. If, for example, it is a 7, place it face up at the bottom of the pile at the 7 o'clock position.

4 Take the card at the top of the pile at 7 o'clock, turn it over and place it at the bottom of the pile at the clock position that matches the number of the card, and so on.

5 The Ace is worth 1, the Jack 11, the Queen 12 and the King goes in the pile at the centre of the clock.

6 To win, you must turn over and place all the cards in the right spot before you have turned over the 4 Kings.

7 If you have turned over the 4 Kings before the end of the game, turn over, one by one, the cards that are still face down in their original piles. If these cards are already in the right place, you win.

THE
DOMINO
EFFECT

Number of Players: 1

What You Need:
- the set of dominos

Object of the Game:
to arrange all the dominos in a row so that when you push the first one, they all fall, one after the other.

RULES OF THE GAME

1 Stand all the dominos up in a row, less than 1 inch (2.5 cm) apart.

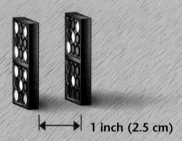

1 inch (2.5 cm)

2 When you have finished, gently push the first domino towards the others and watch them fall, one by one.

Variation:
if you master the technique, you can make more complicated shapes such as curves, zigzags, etc.

Pick-up STICKS

Number of Players: 2

What You Need:
- the *Pick-up Sticks* set

RULES OF THE GAME

1 One player holds all the sticks together in one hand, with the points against the table. The player then opens his or her hand and lets all the sticks fall.

2 Players take turns picking up sticks, one by one, without moving any other stick. A player's turn is over when he or she moves another stick. Any stick a player picked up which caused another one to move is put back into the box and is not counted at the end of the game.

3 Once you have picked up 1 stick, you can use it to pick up others.

Object of the Game:

to get as many points as possible by picking up the sticks.

4 Different coloured sticks have different values (see the table).

5 The game ends when there are no sticks left to pick up. The player with the most points wins.

Variation: try this shorter game; for
each turn, a player drops all the sticks, then picks up as many as possible without moving another stick. The player who picks up the sticks with the most points wins. Try to find the best way of dropping the sticks to get the most points.

STICK VALUES:

black	20 points
yellow	10 points
blue	5 points
red	3 points
green	2 points

Hint: To pick up a stick, press down on the point with the tip of your finger. This will lift the stick and make it easier to pick up without moving the other sticks.

20   10   5   3   2

9

TICK-TACK-TOE

Number of Players: 2
What You Need:
- 2 felt markers
- 1 piece of paper

Object of the Game:
to be the first to make a row of three Xs or three Os, either horizontally, vertically or diagonally.

RULES OF THE GAME

1 Draw a grid on the piece of paper, as shown.

2 One of the players decides to draw Xs, the other Os.

3 Players take turns drawing their letters in the squares, 1 per turn.

4 The first player to draw a row of three Xs or Os wins the game.

THE MAGIC MARKER

Number of Players: 2
What You Need:
- 1 blindfold
- 1 felt marker
- sheets of paper

Object of the Game:
to guess what you have drawn with your blindfold still on.

RULES OF THE GAME

1 One player is blindfolded and given a piece of paper and a marker.

2 The other player takes the blindfolded player's hand and guides it to draw something on the piece of paper.

3 Once the drawing is finished, the blindfolded player must guess what it is.

4 The two players can then switch places and play again.

CAPTURE

Number of Players: 2

What You Need:
- 1 piece of paper
- 2 different coloured felt markers

Object of the Game:
to make as many squares as possible.

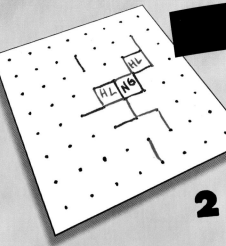

1 One of the players draws a square with 49 dots close together, as shown.

2 Players take turns drawing a line between 2 dots to connect them.

3 The player who closes a square (by drawing the fourth side) writes his or her initials inside it.

4 The game ends when it is impossible to make more squares. The player with the most squares wins.

Number of Players: 2

What You Need:
- 1 piece of graph paper
- 2 different coloured felt markers

Object of the Game:
to write OXO as many times as possible.

RULES OF THE GAME

1 One of the players outlines a large square on the piece of graph paper.

2 Players take turns drawing an X or an O in one of the little squares.

3 Any time a player writes OXO either horizontally, vertically or diagonally, he or she draws a line through the word and gets 1 point. Letters that have been crossed out can still be used to form OXO in other directions.

4 When it is no longer possible to form the word OXO within the large square, the players count their points. The player with the most points wins.

THE FOX

Number of Players: 2
What You Need:
- *The Fox and the Crow* game board
- the 24 illustrated game cards for *The Fox and the Crow*

RULES OF THE GAME

1 The players decide who will be the Fox and who will be the Crow.

2 One of the players shuffles the cards and places them face down (so that the picture is hidden) in a pile on the table.

3 For each turn, pick up a card. If the card shows your character, place it face up on one of the matching squares on the board. In other words, if you are the Crow and you pick up a Crow, place it on a Crow square. If you pick up the other player's character (a Fox), put it on the bottom of the pile of cards.

AND THE CROW

Object of the Game:
to fill all of your squares
on the game board.

4 If you pick up a Cheese card, you must take
one of your cards off the game board and put
it back on the bottom of the pile, and put the
Cheese card aside.

5 The first player to fill all of his or her
squares on the board wins.

123 Pick Up!

RULES OF THE GAME

Number of Players: 2
What You Need:
- 15 sticks from the *Pick-up Sticks* set

Object of the Game: to avoid picking up the last stick.

1 One of the players places the 15 sticks on the table.

2 Players take turns picking up either 1 or 2 or 3 sticks.

3 The player who picks up the last stick loses.

Note: There's a trick to not picking up the last stick. It's up to you to figure it out!

Domino Bandits

Object of the Game: to steal as many dominos as possible.

RULES OF THE GAME

1 Players place all the dominos face down on the table, so that the dots are hidden.

2 Each player picks up a domino. The player who picks the domino with the most dots goes first.

3 For each turn, pick up a domino and place it face up in front of you, so that the dots are visible. Then look at your opponent's dominos. If you see one with the same number of dots on one half as on one half of the domino you have just picked up, you can steal it.

Number of Players: 2
What You Need:
- the set of dominos

4 The game ends when there are no dominos left face down. The player with the most dominos wins.

WAR!

Number of Players: 2

What You Need:
- 52 playing cards

Object of the Game:
to collect all the cards.

RULES OF THE GAME

1 One of the players makes sure that the jokers are removed from the deck, shuffles the cards and deals them all.

2 Players place their cards face down in a pile in front of them.

3 Each player turns over the card on the top of his or her pile and places it in the centre of the table.

4 The player with the highest card takes both cards and puts them aside.

5 There is "war" when both players turn over the same card. The players then continue to turn cards over, one by one, until one player turns over a card of the same value as the first card. That player then picks up all the cards and sets them aside. In other words, if there is "war" between two 10s, the first player to turn over another 10 picks up all the cards turned face up on the table.

6 When you have turned over all the cards in your pile, use the cards that you have set aside to continue the game.

7 If you have no more cards during a "war", the other player must turn over one card for each pile until the "war" is won. The winner takes both piles.

8 The player who collects all the cards wins.

HELP!

Number of Players: 2

What You Need:
- the *Help!* game board
- 6 counters
- 1 die

Object of the Game:
to save the cat.

RULES OF THE GAME

1 Each player chooses 3 counters of the same colour.

2 Players take turns rolling the die. The player who rolls the highest number goes first and picks a side of the board to play on.

3 Place each of your counters on one of the START squares on your side of the board.

4 For each turn, roll the die. You need a 2 or a 5 to advance from START. When you get a 2 or a 5, roll the die again and move up the ladder the number of spaces shown.

5 The first player to reach the cat at the top of the ladder with all 3 counters wins. You need the exact number to reach the top. If the number you get is too high, go down the ladder the remaining number of spaces and try again on your next turn.

Hint: every time you get a 2 or a 5, start moving a different counter up the ladder.

Pickin' Apples

Number of Players: 2
What You Need:
- the *Pickin' Apples* game board
- the 24 illustrated game cards for *Pickin' Apples*
- 1 die

Object of the Game: to be the first to collect 4 Basket cards.

RULES OF THE GAME

1 One of the players separates the cards between Apple cards and Basket cards and places both piles on the table.

3 For each turn, roll the die and pick up the number of Apple cards shown. Place these cards on the spaces on your side of the board.

2 Both players roll the die. The player with the highest number goes first and chooses which side of the board he or she will play on.

4 You must get the exact number to fill the spaces on your side of the board. If the number you get is too high, you must remove the remaining number of cards from your side of the board.

5 When the 8 spaces on your side of the board are filled, remove the cards and put them back in the pile. Then take one Basket card and set it aside.

6 The first player to fill his or her side of the board 4 times and pick up 4 Basket cards, wins.

THE CRAZY NUMBER GAME

Number of Players: 2 to 4

What You Need:
- *The Crazy Number Game* board
- 8 counters for each player, for 2 players
- 4 counters for each player, for 3 or 4 players
- 2 dice

RULES OF THE GAME

1 Players take turns rolling the dice. The player with the highest number goes first.

2 For each turn, roll the dice and add the numbers together. Then place a counter on the space that matches your total. If there is already a counter on that space, don't put your counter on it, instead, pick up the one that's already there.

Object of the Game:
to have counters at the end
of the game.

3 If you get a 7, you must place a counter on space 7 even if there is already one or more counters on it.

4 If you roll doubles, pick up all the counters on space 7 and play again. If there are no counters on space 7, place a counter on the space matching the total as usual, and play again.

5 When you have no more counters, you are out of the game. The game ends when only one player is left with one or more counters. That player wins.

CARD *Thief*

Number of Players: 2 to 4

What You Need:
- 52 playing cards

Object of the Game:
to have the most cards at the end of the game.

RULES OF THE GAME

1 One of the players removes the jokers from the deck, shuffles the cards and deals 4 to every player. The dealer then places 4 cards face up on the table and places the remaining cards face down in a pile in the centre. The player to the left of the dealer goes first.

2 The first player checks if a pair can be made with one of the cards in his or her hand and one of the cards face up on the table. If so, he or she takes both cards and places them in a pile face up, so that the other players can see the card on top. If the player doesn't have a card that matches one on the table, he or she must discard a card, face up on the table.

3 Players then take turns trying to make pairs with cards on the table or with cards on the tops of their opponents' piles. If you have a card that matches the one on top of your opponent's pile, place your card on top and steal the whole pile, and add it to your pile.

4 If you have no more cards left in your hand, pick one from the pile in the centre at the beginning of your turn.

5 If there are no more cards left face up on the table, the dealer turns over 4 new cards from the pile and the game continues.

6 The game ends when players have no more cards in their hands and there are no more cards left in the pile in the centre. The player with the most cards wins.

TIDDLY WINKS

Number of Players: 2 to 4
What You Need:
- **5 counters of the same colour for each player**
- **a small, shallow bowl**

Object of the Game:
to make 4 of your counters jump into the bowl.

1 One of the players places the bowl either on a table cloth or on a carpeted surface.

2 Players sit around the bowl, at equal distances from it.

3 Players take turns trying to make a counter jump into the bowl by pressing another counter onto it, near the edge.

4 The first player to get 4 of his or her counters into the bowl wins.

Snakes AND LADDERS

Number of Players: 2 to 4
What You Need:
- **the *Snakes and Ladders* game board**
- **4 counters of the same colour for each player**
- **1 die**

1 Players take turns rolling the die. The player with the highest number goes first.

2 For each turn, roll the die and advance the number of spaces shown. If you land on a space that is already occupied, go back to where you came from and wait for your next turn. This rule does not apply to the last space on the board.

3 If you land on the bottom of a ladder, climb to the top of it. If you land on the tail of a snake, slide down to its head.

4 You need the exact number to land on the last space. If the number you get is too high, move backwards the remaining number of spaces.

5 The first player to get all his or her counters on the last space wins.

Object of the Game: to get all your counters to the last space.

THE MEMORY GAME

Number of Players: 2 to 4
What You Need:
- 52 playing cards

Object of the Game: to have the most cards at the end of the game.

RULES OF THE GAME

1 One of the players removes the jokers from the deck, shuffles the cards and spreads them out, face down on the table.

2 The player to the left of the dealer goes first, followed by the player to his or her left, and so on.

3 For each turn, turn over 2 cards on the table. If the 2 cards have the same value, pick them up and play again. If the two cards are not the same, turn them over so that they are face down again. Your turn is over.

4 The game ends when there are no more cards left on the table. The player with the most pairs wins.

LUCKY 15

Number of Players: 2 to 4
What You Need:
- 1 die

Object of the Game: to make 15, or as close to 15 as possible without going over, in three rolls of the die or more.

RULES OF THE GAME

1 Players roll the die. The player with the highest number goes first.

2 Each player rolls the die 3 times or more to try to make 15, or as close to 15 as possible without going over.

3 If a player gets exactly 15 in 3 rolls, he or she gets 2 points.

4 If no one gets exactly 15, the player who is the closest to 15 without going over gets 1 point.

5 If a player goes over 15, he or she loses 1 point.

6 If 2 players are tied with the same total, the one with the fewest rolls gets 1 point. If both players are tied after rolling the die the same number of times, neither player gets a point.

7 The first player to get 10 points wins.

MONSTER MADNESS

Number of Players: 2 to 4
What You Need:
- 1 piece of paper for each player
- 1 felt marker for each player

Object of the Game:
to draw crazy monsters!

RULES OF THE GAME

1 Without showing it to the others, each player draws the head and neck of a monster at the top of their piece of paper which has been folded in thirds.

2 Each player then folds their piece of paper so that only the neck is visible and passes the drawing to another player.

3 On the new folded piece of paper, each player draws a body onto the neck and draws the top part of the monster's legs.

4 Players fold the paper again so that only the top part of the legs is visible, then pass the drawings to another player.

5 On the new piece of folded paper, each player draws the rest of the legs and the feet of the monster.

6 Players then unfold the piece of paper and look at the drawings. What crazy-looking monsters!

DOMINOS

Number of Players: 2 to 4

What You Need:
- the set of dominos

Object of the Game:
to get rid of all your dominos as quickly as possible.

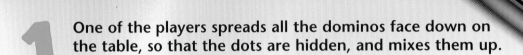

RULES OF THE GAME

1 One of the players spreads all the dominos face down on the table, so that the dots are hidden, and mixes them up.

2 Each player picks up 5 dominos and stands them up in front of them so that the others cannot see the dots. The dominos left face down on the table are the "stock."

3 The player who has the highest "double" places it face up in the centre. (A double is a domino with the same number of dots on both halves.)

4 The next player to the left then tries to match one of his or her dominos to one end of the domino on the table. To match, one of the halves of a domino must be identical to one of the halves of the domino on the table. The domino that matches is placed next to the one on the table, identical halves touching, so that the two dominos form a chain.

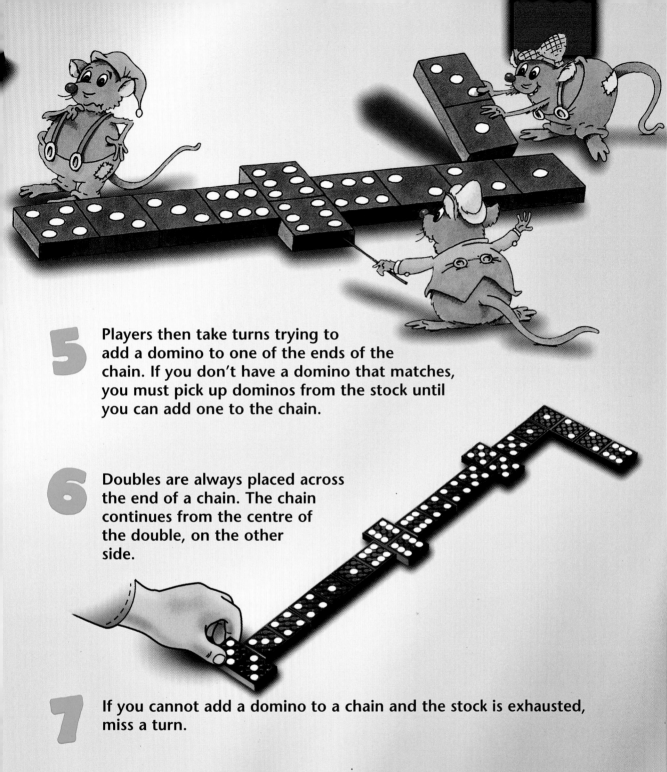

5 Players then take turns trying to add a domino to one of the ends of the chain. If you don't have a domino that matches, you must pick up dominos from the stock until you can add one to the chain.

6 Doubles are always placed across the end of a chain. The chain continues from the centre of the double, on the other side.

7 If you cannot add a domino to a chain and the stock is exhausted, miss a turn.

8 The first player with no more dominos wins. If all the players still have dominos left but cannot add any of them to a chain, players count all the dots on their remaining dominos. The player with the least dots wins. In both cases, the winner gets the number of points counted from the dominos left in the hands of all the other players. The first player to get 100 points wins the match.

Pin the Tail on the DONKEY

Number of Players: 4 or more

What You Need:
- the *Pin the Tail on the Donkey* poster
- adhesive tape or thumbtacks
- 1 numbered donkey tail for each player
- 1 blindfold

Object of the Game:
to place the donkey's tail in the right place.

RULES OF THE GAME

1 One of the players places the poster on the wall with tape or thumbtacks, so that the players can all reach it easily.

28

2 Each player is blindfolded in turn. The other players spin him or her around a few times, then direct the blindfolded player towards the poster.

3 With one hand, the blindfolded player must place the tail on the donkey.

4 The player who places the tail closest to the right spot on the poster wins.

Who am I?

Number of Players: 4 or more

What You Need:
- pieces of paper
- felt markers
- adhesive tape
- the help of an adult

Object of the Game:
to guess what the drawing on your forehead is.

RULES OF THE GAME

1 Before the game begins, an adult must draw different things, animals or characters onto little pieces of paper.

2 The adult then sticks one drawing onto each of the players' foreheads with adhesive tape; players must not see the drawings on their foreheads.

3 When all the players have a drawing on their forehead, they take turns asking each other questions about it to try and guess what it is.

4 You can only answer questions with a yes or no.

5 If you think you know what the drawing on your forehead is, say it to the other players. If you are right, you win. If not, the game continues.

THE OBSERVATION GAME

Number of Players: 4 or more
What You Need:
- 1 piece of paper
- 1 felt marker

Object of the Game:
to identify what has been added or changed on a drawing.

RULES OF THE GAME

1 The players choose one player who will draw the first picture.

2 That player quickly draws something on a piece of paper and shows it to the other players, who can study it for 1 minute.

3 The player then takes the drawing back and, without the other players seeing, adds something else to the drawing or changes it a little.

4 The player then shows it to the others again. The first player to correctly identify what has been added or changed on the drawing wins and draws next.

Charades

Number of Players: 4 or more
Object of the Game:
to guess what is being mimed.

RULES OF THE GAME

1 Players write down, on little pieces of paper, the names of different kinds of animals or types of work, and place them in a bowl.

2 Players decide which of them will start.

3 The first player takes a piece of paper out of the bowl, and mimes the animal or the type of work named on it. The player cannot use words or sounds.

4 The first player to guess what is being mimed wins, and then it is his or her turn to take a piece of paper from the bowl and mime.

Packs of Pairs

Number of Players: 4 or more

What You Need:
- the game cards for the Fox and the Crow
- the game cards for Picking Apples
- 1 die

Object of the Game:
to make as many pairs as possible.

RULES OF THE GAME

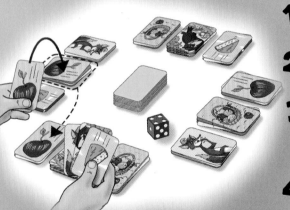

1 One of the players shuffles all the cards together and places them face down in a pile.

2 Players take turns rolling the die. The player with the highest number goes first.

3 For each turn, roll the die and pick up the number of cards shown from the pile. If you get a 6, take 1 card from the player on the left. If that player has no cards, take 1 card from the pile.

4 If you have a pair (2 Crows, 2 Apples, etc.) place it face up in front of you so that the other players can see it. Put all the same pairs together in a pile.

5 You can only put down a pair on your turn. But before you do, check the cards in front of the player to your left. If you find a pair, or a pile of pairs, identical to the one in your hand, you can steal it and put all the pairs down together. But you can only steal before you put down a pair.

6 When there are no more cards in the pile, players take turns taking 1 card from the first player to the left who still has cards.

7 If you have no more cards in your hand, you cannot continue playing. But the player to your right can still steal your pairs, and you can still count your pairs at the end.

8 The game ends when all the cards are in pairs, face up on the table. The player with the most pairs wins.